I0109248

NOTHING
BUT
ITSELF

NOTHING
BUT
ITSELF

poetry by
Diane Lee Moomey

Copyright © 2018 by Diane Lee Moomey

All rights reserved. No part of this book may be reproduced or utilized in any form or by any means, electronic or mechanical, including photocopying, recording, or by any information storage and retrieval system, without permission in writing from the publisher.

Day'sEye Press and Studios
PO Box 628
El Granada, CA 94018
www.dayseyepressandstudios.com

ISBN: 978-0-9619714-8-9

Printed in the United States of America

Cover art copyright 2018 by Diane Lee Moomey

You may contact Diane at dianeleemoomey@gmail.com or through her *Poets and Writers'* page:

www.pw.org/content/diane_moomey

What It Is

These poems are stories, rantings, calls: "Is anybody out there? Does anyone hear me and answer 'yes, this is so'?" Poetry starts at a spot on the edge of a lake and instead of walking around the perimeter to get to the other side, plunges into the water. Once submerged it does not do a sensible crawl across but duck dives, comes up in a spray of bubbles a few yards away, dives again, surfaces again. First the breast stroke, now the back stroke, the butterfly—poetry gains the opposite shore and leaves not a trace of its coming.

Who I'm Thanking:

David E. LeCount
Casey FitzSimons
Steve Cosgrove
Rosemary Ybarra-Garcia
Jerry Dyer
Marvin R. Hiemstra
Kathleen McClung
Caroline Goodwin
Lisa Rosenberg
Erin Redfern
Steve Long
and
The Willow Glen Poets
The Waverley Writers
The Not Yet Dead Poets' Society
and my most beloved
Coastside Poets

MAKING THE WILD
OUR OWN

Weathers

I
Another night wind, wet wind bears
the breaths of owl and cougar, flings
pine limbs down. These crash
to wet ground. Wet hunters
stalk prey,
wet prey,
can't wait.
Dark wet feet. Water howls down
spouts; clay bowls, ivy bowls
smash flat onto bricks. Out there,
dark there, one shriek—something
small. I wrap myself in woolen shawl.

II
A midday sun. All color gone
from cliffs, from sky, from shadows. Empty
doorways—the village sleeps. Waves
of far-off hills break blue on gray
horizons. Tawny stone rises sheer
above this valley floor, its glassy
facets flashing yellow, white.
A raven circles low above
the melting road. I wish
I had another sweater to take off.

Black Friday at the Ocean

Some of us have chosen *not* to heed
the siren call of myriad malls that grace
our land, and cluster now atop the shaggy
bluffs by Pillar Point, tidepools below.
Above's an opalescent sky whose tender

grays I might essay with watercolor;
between, the auburn wings of hunting hawks.
We're families and strangers walking off
yesterday's debauch, perhaps—that day
of too much roasted bird, of good red wine—

some of us accompanied by hounds
plumper than they were on Wednesday, dogs
made round by treats dropped quietly beneath
the crocheted edges of white tablecloths.
Gifts of obligation for the season?

Still waiting to be found, or were bought
this morning on browsers by early risers deep
in second cups of coffee, or may be bought
this evening when sandy shoes are set beside
the back door, laptops opened, dogs collapsed

in gratitude beside the fire. Later.
For now, bright finny boards are ferried up
and down the crumbling slopes, a girl in yellow
tutu climbs a cypress tree and seekers
of shellfish forage on the rocks following

the tide which, today, will reach
its nadir at 2:22 pm exactly.

Sardines are running,

                  says the stranger, pointing,
while in low surf, eight curved backs
bob at fish we cannot see. Nearly
close enough to touch—the soft black
fins, the almost-smile—dolphins
trolling north toward the harbor, perhaps
aware of being watched.

Sardines, she says again, she
one of a line of us, strangers, talking
to each other, telephoto
lenses and camera phones
in hand,
our sandy
walks paused: the wild,
for once, comes close to land
and we strangers smile

and click as we do for our children
splashing in the shallows; point and click,
wanting
to make the Wild our own.

Raven, Two Views

I
Alone, its kind
shunning the gregarious life
of crows, its sparse cries
bringing no reply, raven circles
between street and chaparral—
now closed, night-dark atop
a power pole, now flashing silver
above creosote bush, now back
to land on wires, swaying.

II
Parked car at the curb, raven
clings with yellow feet
to the narrow ledge holding
the driver's window in place,
topples, nearly falls, flaps
wings, balances, beak pressed
close to its shadow self
in the glass. Pressed close and, yes,
talking.

Ode to a Hairy Caterpillar With Red Spots

I did not mean to kill you.

Not that your tufted spines are dear to me,
for in truth they may be poisoned,
and not that your presence in this moment,
on my deck, in this pot, on this leaf,
is welcome in any way, your mandibles
making lace of my camellias, but

I did not need to kill you,
did not mean to kill you,
only meant to scoop you

between two leaves and drop you
over the railing into the softest of ivies
to a new life. Meant that, but you

fell from the rescue leaf and hit the deck,
rolled into the crack between two boards.
You'd have tumbled to the bricks below
but for a daring midair twist
that glued you to the crack's sheer side
as if you'd planned it.

I did not mean to kill you,
and
I did not.

Once during the drought,

                              that long
drought, during one of those
late post-daybreak dreams you swear
are what you're waking into, I heard
a dripping from the upstairs
deck onto my own—a pattering of drops
sliding between the planks to fall
onto fuchsia and sedum, the hollow
echo of drops as they hit the downspouts
debouching onto paths below—

and through my half-closed eyes
the light seemed dull enough for that.
So I believed in the power of the rain dance
I'd done the day before and lay there,
not engaging

in the reality of bright sun on the decking,
the upstairs neighbors taking
their showers.

Pigeon Point

We leaned
against a railing that shook
beneath our jacketed elbows, leaned
watching dolphins arc their ways
past us toward the beach behind
as if nothing on earth or sea
were more important and of course,
nothing is. We leaned

against a wooden fence at the land's
end of our world, a split rail
hanging over iceplant and crooked trail,
watched Nikeed hikers follow it down-
to an improbable beach below. We spoke,

facing whitecaps, of what is terribly
important to us in our seventh decade,
spoke facing the place where the dolphins
had come through, fought
as we sometimes do, thought

they *could* have been porpoises.

NEVER THINK OF FALLING

First Friend

First grade—walking home the long
way because along that way are new
daffodils. Today we'll play
at your house. Deep

in your maple shade, we eat Oreos
and fondle plump pink valentines
on feathery stalks. (Your mother
calls these flowers *bleeding*
hearts, but they don't.)

We talk of fairies—*are there
any?* You think not.

Your baby brother wants
your lap, and hits me on the head
with his new garden trowel.

I cry. You kiss
the hurt spot, make better.

Her Screen' Porch

has a wicker chair with yellow chintz
that's curved to fit her, cabbage roses curved
to fit her—the mother's mother. Wooden floor
was red, then blue, then green, now red again
—its peeling paint reveals the layers, fancies

of the farmer's wives, the mother's mother's
mothers gone before—repainted every
other spring. That floor now sags beneath
the weight of all their decades: every mother,
having daily laundered, pickled, scrubbed,

would leave her steamy kitchen, take her hour
in a wicker chair to peer through wire
mesh once-taut across its wooden frame.
She'd see who's walking hand in hand and who's
alone, who's got a baby carriage. Summer

days, I'd visit. Summer evenings, call
to supper. Sticky hands, child's hands
slapped that screen door open, slammed it closed
again—*Don't slam the door! Wash your hands,*
Take a plate! Stop running! Running 'round

the ell of porch cornering the house
to table set behind the vine of Dutchman's
Pipe, our privacy from street and yellow
jackets. Eat out there and sleep out there—
the rusty screen's sufficient buffer from

the darkest dangers of *those* summer nights.

Salsa

I said to God—
yes, I did, bold as paint I said—
I know you, yes, indeed I do, and God
didn't answer.

Then I said. *I know you, you smell
like chips and salsa,* said

*I know your voice, I get messages
from you on my cellphone
all the time.*

When you pass by—yes, I know
it's you—dust falls from your coat
and lands on my own sleeve. Dust

may be all I ever see of you,
but that could be enough.

Sunrise Service

She'd walked to church,
ten blocks or so through pre-dawn
Easter streets, surprised to be allowed
to walk alone, now
old enough—and joined
the service not in pews
but in the parking lot on new
folding chairs, facing east.

She'd walked to church in white
gloves—one wore white gloves—and sat
not listening to the pastor but watching fat
cloud banks like far-off forests, those
and a mackerel sky. A gilded mackerel sky
behind which she knew shone
the eye of God.

First Date

No snow,
but we've walked home
from school, so—spring.
Or fall. At the Rexall's

on Fleming Road,
on red plastic stools at the yellow counter
you buy me the ten cent cherry Coke.
For yourself, the five, since all you have
is fifteen cents.

We are each eleven, and count the time
between our birthdays. I
am younger by two months.

Then to my house and the couch
in our garage, the one with broken
springs, the couch that soon
will be Goodwill's, but not today.

We jump and jump
until the dog goes crazy
and my mother calls out the window
it's time for you to go home.

One last bounce. You say
you've never had so much fun
in your whole life.

Climbing to the Ceiling of the Gym

Left hand, right hand pull her up; both
feet cup the wrist-thick rope and push;
sisal prickles like a cowhide—
bristles strip the tender skin from child

thighs bare below the hems of blue
shorts. Gym mats thin and few beneath—
she doesn't think of falling. Every day
that length, calling. All the way, slap

the rafter, down again—resist the urge
to slide—she lets herself descend, ignores
admiring glares from other kids. That length—
enticing. Maybe on the hundredth climb

she'll smack that beam, a trap door will fly open
—wide, flat roof!—and she'll shuffle
sneakered feet through gravel, lift her arms
and soar away, like Wendy, above the chimneys
of Detroit.

Wearing Snakes

I let them wrap around my wrists, the sleek
green scales so like the gold link
bracelet Mother wears to parties. So like—
I close my eyes while wearing one and feel

the other. In summer's green beside the fence,
by long stems my father's mower doesn't
reach, I wait and place my wrist on mullein,
grasses, dock. They part. I intercept

and lift, feel it wrap. Snake will twine
around an arm, always: body taut
and steadying itself against a fall.
(Ruby tongue flicks in and out). In my

own world I am, (ruby tongue tastes),
the only little girl who wears snakes.

LIGHTS ABOVE
THE POLES

Brie

I'm opening a Brie for you. I'll set
it where its shoulders, creamy firm, will slump
into the warmth of afternoon, and where
what breeze there is today will carry news
of "Brie" out to the highway, where you may

be driving. Yo-Yo Ma is at full volume
now (in case you're walking by), and I've
opened my Neruda to the verse
that seemed to summon you a time or two
ago, and read its final stanza twice,

read aloud his final stanza twice.
And I have trimmed the ivy, cut the spent
camellia blossoms, swept the brown ones from
beneath the pots that cluster near the door
where surely you will knock and bring a poem,

like you did before.

Nigiri

I thought we'd have more days.

I seem to be mistaking a night-bird's voice
for yours, and a branch, roof-fallen,
for a knock upon my door. I'm fooled
by light and shadows on a wall—mere light
and shadow and by words I think are meant
for my ears, by a crescent moon I take for ours,
by the children of others.

You set the last nigiri on my plate
and filled my cup. I thought
we'd have more days.

Forty-Three and One-Half . . .

after Edna St. Vincent Millay

But I remember *every* lip, and where,
and *all* the hands that ever cupped my cheek;
recall the day and season bringing each
and bearing each away: Our mingled hair,
an arm across me in the night, the wary
promises we may have meant to keep;
remember canyons far too wide to leap
and lips, unkissed, that smiled across. This heart

has been no wide equator—endless vine
and leaf whose suns move gently south to north,
timeless zone of valleys, bowls of verdant
fruit—but is the sleepless summer, time
between the thaw and freeze, brief bringing forth
of tiny berries, lights above the poles.

Moon, Moon

A waxing moon, near full. Your patio—
camellia petals spread about our feet,
the light, two shadows clear on yellow stucco
walls. Our speech—the cadences that nearly
sweep away the memory of distance,
of other marriages, of years estranged.
Almost, I could believe in second chance,
another answer. But I flew away

alone, and brought a pebble home—so round,
so like another moon. Camellia jar
with saucer overflowing on the ground,
the splashing echoing your words. I see
my solitary shadow on the wall,
remember all you told me of your dream.

Thirty Below

Beneath the borealis we are wrapped
in down and Dacron, glove in glove. Our love
tonight's an argument about intent:
You name this radiance Divine, with rapt

attention point out Heaven's lights, and speak
of Gabriel enthroned above the Pole,
angelic trumpeting, a shimmering
that knows itself and you. I must critique,

and speak of plasma and electrons blind
as stones on pavement; senseless protons, photons,
solar winds. And on I talk. You balk;
we're kept apart by more than gloves tonight.

I think I'd give the whole of what is mine
to hear a single word from your Divine.

Epiphany

No king came riding to the door this morning
dressed in cloth of gold, no magus robed
in deeper thought; nor shepherds, country men
with woolen robes askew from sleeping rough

in fields made hard with winter. None arrived
with frankincense. But brief, a flash within
my darkened skull that *might* have been the light
of morning only, blinds left slightly open,

fog of sleep—but I'll believe it was
the nova of your own, your sweet, verily
your sweet and baby face, smiling,
come to bless in spite of all I'd left

undone. You smiling, saying *yes,*
we did okay in spite of all. Yes.

Love at the Laundromat

Her dollar bills convert themselves to dimes,
a tear for every silvery *clunk* into
the pot below the spout. Who will keep

the flat? His frowns, his quarters, his fingers hover
over buttons labeled *Tide, All,*
Breeze—*All* falls into the tray.

Towels, sheets, detergent, quarters—lids
slamming, distant seats, separate papers,
breaking-up suspended for the nonce

although their audience of pensioners,
of students, single fathers, mothers-of-three
and cellphone users wouldn't notice. More

clink of dimes and quarters—spinning yellow
sheets, the aqua towels, the tumbling, stopping,
folding. It does take two to fold a sheet.

Corner to corner, finger to finger, never
looking at him; and corner to corner, never
looking at her. He says *please let's*

not buy new sheets. Hand
to hand, he says *let's go home*
and dirty up the old ones. Don't

cry. And so they don't, they do, she doesn't,
(not for awhile, anyway), and that was that.

Ode, with Wings

Had I loved you as a farmer, a farmer,
I'd have to drive all day
 for just a glimpse of you
across your lower pasture,
deep in wheat grass, deep. Instead

you flew me upside down.

Had I loved you as a fisherman, a fisherman,
I'd need to row all night
to find the place we last dropped anchor,
and with a glass, the perfect glass,
might see your nets. Instead,

you flew me upside down. Instead,

I loved you in the air, the air. You wore
new wings, and in your father's plane
so proudly lent, you flew me upside down.
Because I loved you there, all skies

belong to you. No need
to drive, to row. Every sky belongs to you.

GIVING YOUR
CLOTHES AWAY

Matroyshka

Your darkling melanoma casts
its shadow over all. You say
that healing's happening—your last
tests lie. (I turn my face

aside, avoid your eyes.) Today
your doctor says you qualify
for hospice, better not to wait.
You say he lies, avoid my eyes.

Your son and daughter will come by.
They're taking you to Europe soon,
or Mexico—the latest trials
are promising!—and you'll refuse

to make a will. (My love for you
affords no place to hide.) To sign
would mean declaring you *approve,*
you give *permission* to be dying.

You're making plans for Mardi Gras
next year—(My tears will come, they'll go)—
your daughter's in the room comparing
fares. New Orleans, perhaps. Or Rio.

Coming Back

No sign upon your ten white
steps, mica-specked, nor on the fossil
rock beside them; nothing
written on the bell that, ringing,
should have brought you to me.
No omen in your invitation—days ago,
the flowered card—and so
through door-glass curved
with age, I watch you, stunned:
your bird-arms rise stiff as if
with cold, in what could be a wave.

You're brittle in your leather
chair, your red chair. Your stick arms—
so brown and dry beneath
your off-the-shoulder dress, so brave—
rise again, embrace me, erase our years
of silence. Embrace me as if as usual,
here at the end of them.

Your legs—careful, like herons
walking, stalking the pools
of your pain. Your bird's beak
nose, sharp enough now to shatter
the egg of the end of your life and hatch
you out somewhere far
beyond *my* reach.

Keeping Your Seat

Curtain falls, curtain call,
houselights rise, patrons rise and blink—

you keep your seat. Slow feet
fill the aisles, spill through double doors
toward a rain-bright street,
stroll out for late drinks

and pastries. Faint horns, the hiss of brakes,
far-off complaints of cab and bus—you
in plush velvet. You may think
the curtain will rise once more, you sink

deeper. The silence! You
could sleep here. The cleaners
might not notice you
as they come through
sweeping spills, spent tickets, last
of the caramel corn, you

low in your seat, no
particular place to go.

A Day Late

No difference. It might have made
no difference at all to have come
on Thursday, when tubes still ferried
molecules of O2 into your nose.
(Not enough—your fingers blue
with lack because by Thursday
there could never be enough.)

It might have made no difference
to have uttered my goodbyes to your closed eyes
instead of through the cellphone the nurse
held to your ear. Or that on Friday
those tubes were rolled into a ball. (I pushed them all
beneath your empty mattress.)

No difference at all,
except that had I come on Thursday,
my goodbyes done, I could have lain, dumb beast,
beside your bed.

Waiting

Because there'll be no beeping
in the middle of another call to tell me
you've fallen again; because

your demands for more Depends
(the long ones in the yellow box)
will not again disrupt the rants, my sister's
and mine, our rants—*do you know
what Mom said to me?*—and your beep
will no longer break into

my business with the bank
or my terror of your abyss and you won't
tell me how much you love me and how
you're not afraid. Because now
no call will come from hospice, ever,
I'm canceling call waiting.

Afterward

I remove my shoes and the day
spreads out ahead of me, curiously
unfilled by myriad joggers in hoodies
and earbuds, the strollers, small dogs
on leashes. A neap tide pulls lightly
at my heels.

Later I say *yes* to tod mun
at the Thai place beside
the esplanade. This evening is cool
and empty around the edges.

Tomorrow will be soon enough
to give your clothes away.

Yellow Line

Across the yellow line, the childish run—
nothing to be done. The yellow bus:
the scent of school that lingers even here
so many miles from gaily-painted walls
where crayon-lettered posters show the lives

of monarch butterflies. Cars and trucks,
the black and yellow bus. The country road—
houses, barns, and chores await, perhaps
a batch of eggs about to hatch—a sight
worth running for. Beside the dotted line

a pickup truck; a gray sedan behind,
blind, catches her in flight and nothing's
to be done. She's lying on her back,
her shoulders small and soft. The gravel's hard
beneath my feet—I watch, and someone strokes

her fingers, curled as if in sleep. We wait,
the witnesses: for twirling lights, for the opening
of double doors, for questioning.
We witnesses, beside the yellow bus
so many miles away from colored walls,
crepe paper flowers.

Angel Wing

An angel met me on the stairs,
and brushed me with one wing—one day
I'll fall to meet my shadow.
So much remains unwritten.

She brushed me with one wing,
I thought you were another.
So much remains unwritten and
my poet soon will leave me.

She thought I was another.
Yes, once I was a changeling.
My poet soon will leave me and
I feel the change of season.

I may have been a changeling.
My poet left these pages. Now
I feel the change of season.
In this I'm not mistaken.

My poet left these pages. Since
they could all be lost (and
I feel I'm not mistaken),
won't you take them with you?

All pages will be lost when
I fall to meet my shadow.
Won't you take them with you?
An angel's met me on the stairs.

MAKING FOR
HIGHER GROUND

Drought

You could, fed up
with red and blue flashing lights
and sickened by the siren howls
of human misery that never stop, *could*
slip through any window and follow
the thread back to Narnia.

You could backtrack your own trail
and know that, had you turned north
in 1981 instead of west, he might
have said *yes* and you might now
be sitting in a different chair.

Or not.
Or you could, reflecting upon lawns
and empty lakes and on the vanishings
of certain birds, either slide into a glass
with ice or, ranting, take to the streets.
And by now, both those roads will lead
to the same place.

It's been such a long drought. So many
things were never born.

Suburbs

Wild things come down from dry hills
to land on roofs, and a ginger cat
slinks beneath a hedge.

Somewhere in the village, a staple
has worked loose from wire netting. Rabbits,
restless, rustle their bedding and wild things

come down from the hills, take cover
between garage and garbage cans.

On a patio, drip lines curve from pot
to pot. Celadon frogs cross cracked earth
to slide under the aspidistra.

Roses twine between houses, black-tailed
deer take refuge. Wild things watch
from the dark below porches. Chickens

seek the safety of the street.

Water Above, Water Below
I Ching, Hexagram #29, K'an K'an: Danger

The lights are going out, dear—one
by one. Circuits short. Listen! The crack

of lines downed, drowned by water rising
from the dark beneath our feet. Wicks,

damp, go limp, collapse in lipid puddles,
hissing. Flashlights flicker, fail in swamps

new-made by dams broken, oaths broken.
Water goes where water will, filling:

water mixed with gas, soaking wood,
bringing to the surface pestilence

once hidden. Listen! Filaments of bulbs—
bright, those wires thin as hairs—now snap.

Tungsten ringlets droop. One shakes the glass
in disbelief, hears only tinkling

within. The lamps are going out, dear
—one by precious one. It's for us

to choose to live in darkness or, blind
and trembling, make for higher ground

and set ourselves alight.

Final Blue

It's not that thoughts of being dead
alarm me, but that berries
bloom along my arms, created by the touch
of rose thorn. Yesterday
my young one eyed those scarlet lakes
like snakes. Not

terror of the Styx, but of the slope
above that shore and not the high
rough water but the certain slide
into it, my nights abiding close to home. Not

the dread of falling into dark
but simply falling: platform heels
I'll never try again, the bicycles. Of feeling
like old furniture, seams come apart,

left curbside. Not
punishment I fear but joking, here:
the blasphemies of bladder making cheer,
all this displacing sex (and even
talk of sex) but not the longing. Not

(believe my lie), of silence in the tomb,
but of the shadow on the skin, the bloom
of deep cyan that creeps from fingers,
lips, and nose, and, oh,
the sparse and silver hair
down there.

Stellar

Suns fling light into space,
spending all they have,
hoping for the chance to
shine on You.

Dark stars,
lacking such light,
instead grow massive,
fat with new matter,
hoping to pull You near
by gravity alone.

Atoms spin
in frenzied dance, hoping
in this way,
to attract Your attention.

You see? We all want You.

Not

Someone wrote: *God*
is not tame.

You are not tame.
You breathe, and thunder rolls.
You move—the earth
quakes and rivers change course,
mountains slide into seas.
Stars shatter into dust—delicious,
even my fear. I do not ask
to be spared, only to know You better.

Cusp

So now—when silence reigns upstairs,
demanding voices stilled by sleep
and quiet dreams, when in this bare

and empty midnight every cup,
for once, is washed and rinsed, each mote
of dust swept up, the missing buttons

found and sewn and every weed
dispatched—the edge between tomorrow
and today rolls smooth beneath

my fingers. Now I can beleive
in magma melting stone, in caves
of water miles below my feet.

And yes, I do believe I hear
the sigh of passing space, my planet
cycling, cycling
at dizzy speed around the sun.

Yet More Thanks

1888 Center for first publishing "What It Is" (original title "Why We Write")

Ascent Aspirations for "Afterward," "Coming Back" and "Once During the Drought"

Blood & Bourbon Press for "Blue" and "A Day Late"

Cæsura for "Suburbs," "Wearing Snakes," "Matroyshka" and "Water Above, Water Below"

California Quarterly for "Podiatria" and "Love at the Laundromat"

Mezzo Cammin for "Cusp," "Her Screen Porch," "Yellow Line," "Forty-Three and One-Half" and "Moon, Moon"

Nature Writing for "Weathers," *Sardines are Running"* and "Raven: Two Views"

Peacock Journal for "Brie," "Thirty Below", "Ode, With Wings", "Pigeon Point" and "Black Friday at the Ocean"

Perfume River Poetry Review for "Angel Wing" and "Climbing to the Ceiling of the Gym"

Plum Tree Tavern and *Portside* for "Drought"

PoeTalk for "Nigiri"

The Road Not Taken for "Epiphany"

Time of Singing for "Salsa," "Sunrise Service" "Stellar" and "Not"

Your Daily Poem for "First Friend" and "First Date"

Origami

Paper square is folded,
folded and look: a bird.

Unfold and back to square,
then fold again. Another bird—
across each face, the fold lines
of the last one.

Nothing but itself.

www.ingramcontent.com/pod-product-compliance
Lightning Source LLC
Chambersburg PA
CBHW060201070426
42447CB00033B/2249